Screen printing on fabric

Screen Printing on Fabric

Valerie Searle
and Roberta Clayson

Studio Vista London

Watson-Guptill Publications New York

© Valerie Searle and Roberta Clayson 1968
Published in London by Studio Vista Limited
Blue Star House, Highgate Hill, London N19
and in New York by Watson-Guptill Publications
165 West 46th Street, New York 10036
Distributed in Canada by General Publishing Co. Ltd
30 Lesmill Road, Don Mills, Toronto, Ontario
Library of Congress Catalog Card Number 68-13121
Set in Univers 9 and 8 point
by V. Siviter Smith and Co. Ltd, Birmingham
Printed in the Netherlands
by N.V. Grafische Industrie, Haarlem
SBN 289.36896.0

Contents

Fig. 1 A Persian wood block *Peacock*

Introduction

Screen printing has evolved from the craft of block printing which dates back to prehistoric times. The main centres of block-printing in the ancient world were China, Persia and India and it is still used as a method of printing textiles in Persia and India. A form of screen printing with metal stencils was practised in Japan in the fourth and fifth centuries AD and screen printing is the combination of block printing and stenciling. Whereas in block printing the colour and pattern are stamped onto the cloth with carved wooden blocks, in screen printing the colour is forced through specially prepared stencils (figs 1 and 2).

Screen printing is now one of the main processes used in industry for the decoration of material. It is possible to reproduce in the home several of the industrial methods and most of the materials suggested in this book can be collected around the home. Only the dyes and some materials included in the more complicated processes have to be bought from printing firms. These are listed on pages 11 and 100.

Designing flat pattern and transferring the pattern on to the material are processes which need to be experimented with and although neither process is difficult, it is necessary to understand the method thoroughly before attempting to produce any of the articles listed below.

Pattern designing is governed by personal preferences and the design methods described in Chapter 4 are aids to developing these preferences as well as an attempt to show the variety of pattern and texture it is possible to produce in screen printing.

Three main methods of transferring designs onto screens are described in this book. Shellac screens are ideal for quick prints, but for more professional results and crispness of detail it is advisable to use either the Profilm or photographic methods.

The variety of objects that can be decorated with screen printing ranges from decorative wall-hangings and greeting-cards through clothing materials and head scarves to household objects such as curtains, bedspreads, wallpapers, table-mats and napkins.

Fig. 2 A Persian wood block *Cone*

1 Basic equipment

The printing table

A normal kitchen table is adequate for printing small objects such as table-napkins or head scarves, but when printing a two or three yard length for curtains or bedspreads it is sensible to use a table of the same length as the material. Also the width of the table must vary according to the width of the material being used. If it is 48" wide the table should be at least 50" wide. A trestle table which can be varied in length or width when necessary is the most suitable table for large pieces of material.

Table covering

Two layers of table covering are necessary to ensure clean and even printing:
1 Cover the table with a thick blanket, pinning it firmly underneath the table with drawing pins (thumbtacks). The blanket must be stretched without a wrinkle.
2 Cover the blanket with American cloth, oil cloth, or thin rubber sheeting, again pinning it firmly underneath the table, ensuring that it is absolutely smooth.

The printing screen

The printing screen is a simple oblong wooden frame. Plain, un-carved picture frames make ideal screens. It is advisable to collect several screens of different sizes as your designs will continually vary in size. There must not be any nails or other sharp projections on the screen, so ensure that the sides are absolutely smooth before use. Also make certain that the screen is not warped because warping causes bad printing and it is difficult to cover the screen correctly.

Organdie

Cotton organdie can be bought by the yard and is the ideal material for covering screens. Do not buy nylon organdie as it is inclined to make the squeegee slip during printing.

Squeegee

The dye is pulled across the screen with the squeegee. This like the screens, can either be bought ready made or constructed very simply in the home (fig. 3).

Nail together two L-shaped pieces of wood, with a strip of rubber $\frac{1}{4}''$ thick in between, allow the rubber to protrude 1'' from between the pieces of wood (figs 3a and b).

The squeegee must always be at least an inch wider than the design and an inch narrower than the screen.

Fig. 3 A diagram of a squeegee
(a) cross section (b) full view

Brown gummed paper

Brown gummed paper is used to strengthen the edges of the screen and to form dye-wells.

The best width to use is 2 inches. This paper is also useful for patching small tears in the screen.

Further essential equipment would be drawing pins (thumb-tacks) staple gun and staples (fig. 4), and remember, whether designing or printing, it is always advisable to have plenty of rags and newspaper for cleaning the printing table and the screen.

Fig. 4 Screen frame, squeegee, staple gun, brown gummed paper, staple remover

Dyestuffs and commercial products

Dyes for fabrics

1 Tinolite pigment dyes, which are marketed by Winsor and Newton Ltd (in the UK and by Geigy Chemical Co. in the USA) as the 'Printex' range of colours. In England these are obtainable in small quantities, where the pigment is already mixed with the Printing binder, and will be ready for immediate use. Pigments and binder can also be bought separately – so that the colours can be mixed with the binder to any strength required.

The standard binder for general use is Tinolite printing binder CM 18% (UK), or Tinolite binder 760 (USA), not available in small quantities.

Preparation of printing paste

A 4 oz. coffee jar will hold enough printing paste to print 3 yards of 48" wide fabric. Add pigment to binder until the required colour is obtained. It is advisable to mix the printing paste in an enamel or plastic bowl so that it can be thoroughly stirred.

When not in use these printing pastes should be kept in tightly closed containers. They will keep indefinitely in good storage conditions, away from excessive heat and protected from frost.

The best results are obtained by printing on cotton and viscose rayon, but these pigment dyes also print satisfactorily on silk and synthetic fibres such as nylon and terylene (polyester). They are not, however, suitable for printing on wool.

Fixing of finished prints

1 Good ventilation is necessary for the efficient drying of the fabric.
2 The printed fabric is then 'fixed' by a simple heat treatment, such as ironing. This is explained more fully in Chapter 3.

Helizarin Dyes (UK) Accolite Dyes (USA)

Recipe:
30 parts Helizarin colour
350 parts binder D

580 parts reduction binder
20 parts urea 1 : 1 of water
20 parts Condensola 1 : 1 of water

Or

1½ dessertspoons of Helizarin colour

17½ dessertspoons of binder D

29 dessertspoons of reduction binder

1 dessertspoon of urea (1:1 of water)

1 dessertspoon of Condensola (1:1 of water)

N.B. (1:1 of water) = (1 teaspoon urea 1 teaspoon water)

1 Mix binder D and reduction binder
2 Mix urea and Condensola
3 Stir mixtures 1 and 2 together
4 Finally add Helizarin colour

Helizarin or Accolite dyes are most suitable for printing on cotton. When printing on synthetic fibres with these dyes special binders must be used.

A 'binder' is used partly as a thickening agent and partly to 'bind' the dyestuff together. The simplest binder is 'starch'.

Dyes for use on paper

Dylon (Tintex, US) dyes or any household dyes are suitable for colouring paper. These dyes are supplied in powder form, and should always be dissolved in a little hot water before adding the rest of the water.

1 Mix in a small quantity of hot water to make sure the powder is thoroughly dissolved.
2 Then add cold water to obtain the required shade.

Basic dyes

These dyes are brilliant colours but tend to fade and wash out when used on fabric. They are excellent, however, for colouring paper. As basic dyes are very concentrated, a teaspoonful of dyestuff mixed in a pint of water should give a strong enough colour. Mix these dyes in the same way as Dylon (or Tintex) dyes described above.

A printing paste for paper prints

By adding a thickening agent to Dylon (Tintex) dye or basic dye, they can easily be made into a printing paste. This printing paste can be used instead of fabric dyes for experimental screen prints on paper because fabric dyes are more expensive.

Thickening agents

A recommended thickening agent is 'Rex' cold water paste powder or any wallpaper paste. It is both cheap and easy to prepare.

1 Fill a large mixing bowl with cold water.

2 Sprinkle the paste powder into the water, stirring constantly so that no lumps form.

3 Keep on adding the paste powder until the mixture becomes thick and creamy.

4 Finally add the dyestuff to the paste, and the mixture is ready for printing.

Fig. 5 Useful kitchen equipment (a) double boiler (b) pint measure (c) mixing bowl (d) dye container (e) spatula (f) whisk (g) decorator's brush

Table Adhesives
Special gum preparations for sticking cloth to the printing table.

Gum Arabic: 500 parts of gum Arabic powder—stirred into 500 parts of cold water.

Bring the mixture to the boil, and leave it overnight to blend. It is now ready for application to the printing table as described in Chapter 3.

A recommended semi-permanent table adhesive is Lankro. The solvent is white spirit or turps substitute.

The adhesive is smoothed on to the printing table with a squeegee as described in Chapter 3. Remember that, unlike gum Arabic, Lankro is not soluble in water and the squeegee and the table will have to be cleaned immediately after use with white spirit or turps substitute.

Shellac solution

This can be obtained in the form of 'knotting' or 'French polish' or shellac in the USA.

This solution has many uses in screen making and printing, which will be explained in the following chapters. The solvent for shellac solution is methylated spirit (alcohol).

Copal varnish

After using the profilm or photographic methods described in Chapters 4 and 5. Varnish is used both as a patching and strengthening agent. The solvent is turps substitute.

Water bound printing inks

These can be used for:
1 Inking lino blocks
2 Monotypes.
3 Rubbing on newsprint.
4 Painting on glass.
5 String and felt prints.

Black cellulose lacquer or screen block out lacquer (solvent: lacquer thinners), or quick drying enamel paint (solvent: turps).

Lacquer is used to paint the positive design onto the screen as described in Chapter 5.

2 Designing

Fig. 6 Flower design from tissue paper collage

Materials for designing

Variety of papers
    cartridge (drawing) paper
    newsprint
    coloured papers
    coloured tissue paper
Paint brushes
    hoghair (bristle), and sable
    2″ wide decorator's brush
    4″ wide decorator's brush
Coloured chalks
Coloured wax crayons
Candles
Paraffin wax
Poster paints
Pencils
Rulers
Yardstick
Assorted waste materials
    match-boxes,
    cotton reels (spools),
    bottle tops etc.

Potatoes
Water-based printing inks
String
Felt
Lino and cutting tools
Wood blocks
Glass (from old photographs
    or window panes)
Household dyes eg.
    Dylon (Tintex)
Household starch
Household bleach
Pipe cleaners
Ink
Pens
Cow gum
Drawing pins (thumbtacks)
Evostick or Bostik (UK)
Elmer's Glue or Sobo (USA)
    semi-permanent waterproof
    glue
Rags and newspapers

Textile designing is essentially the creating of two-dimensional patterns on material, but as most materials are draped when in use, the patterns must also work three dimensionally. Therefore the design must enhance not detract from the drape of the material. The different textures and weights of material must also be considered. It is not possible to use the same design for silk as for hessian (burlap). The qualities of the textiles are too different.

When designing it is always important to keep in mind the effect of the finished printed material. Never use a design with a strong, one-way diagonal as this has an unbalancing effect when the material is draped.

Remember that complete shapes on the flat material will be broken when the material is draped (figs 7 and 8).

Variations within a design can be obtained by changing the direction of the screen while printing. In this way a simple repeat can become part of a larger composite one (figs 9, 10, 11 and 12). But this kind of designing must always be worked out within the

width of material being used. For example, if the material is 48"
wide, two of the composite repeats will fit into the width if the
original repeat is 12" wide.

Fig. 7 Undraped fabric

Fig. 8 Draped fabric showing
broken shapes

Fig. 9 A simple design repeat

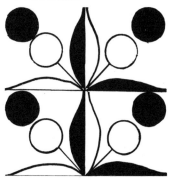

Fig. 10 Variations of composite
repeats

Geometric designs

Geometric designs in bright clear colours are simple to draw and
effective when printed.

The variety of shapes and combinations of shapes is enormous
and by varying the size of the designs, they can be used for any
texture or weight of material. Geometrical designs can be built-up

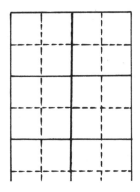

Fig. 11 Variations of composite repeats

Fig. 12 Table registration for composite repeat

from textured paper, paper collage or textured paper from experimental screens (see Chapter 4).

Designs from plant drawing

By far the most popular designs in furnishing or dress fabrics are floral. Probably because flowers and plants have an inherent rhythm which naturally enhances the fabric. The structure and colour of a plant or flower are an ideal starting point for a design. A perfect plant drawing is difficult to achieve, but for basic designing, perfection of drawing is not always necessary. Before attempting to draw a plant, study it carefully. Every plant or flower has an individual structure and shape and when portraying a specific plant it is this basic structure that pin-points its character. It is not necessary to use an entire plant or flower as a basis for designing. Leaves or petals are just as effective and are not so difficult to work into a design (fig. 13).

Fig. 13 Design based on a drawing of corn

Fig. 14 Textured paper and newspaper used in a collage design

Fig. 15 Diagrams showing the stages of overlaying tissue paper, first colour yellow

Fig. 16 Second colour blue

Fig. 17 Third colour green, formed by the first two colours

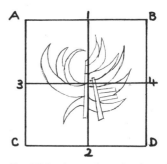

Fig. 18 Putting an irregular shaped collage design into repeat

Collage

A simple definition of collage is the combining of shapes, torn or cut out of paper or material into a co-ordinated pattern. Collage can either be used to build up abstract designs based entirely on texture or stylised designs on plant drawings (fig. 14).

The type of design created depends on the materials used. Designs from coloured tissue paper are delicate, as the transparency of the tissue paper allows the layered colours to shine through one another. When printing the design onto material the same effect can be obtained by overprinting one colour onto another (figs 15, 16, 17 and 19).

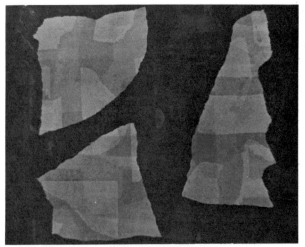

Fig. 19 Design made with overlaid tissue paper

Dye-washed paper, newspaper and paper textured with printing ink are all raw materials for a collage.

It is sometimes difficult to work the irregular shapes into an evenly measured design. There are several ways of overcoming this.

1 Form the collage within a regular simple shape, for example a circle or hexagon. The collaged shapes then become the main motif of a design.

2 Having decided on the size of one repeat of the design, work the collage to within 2 inches of the inside edge of the repeat. Then cut the repeat two ways, along the width and the length (fig. 18).

Match the top and the bottom edges and the two sides as you would do with an ordinary repeat.

3 Work a large area of collage (2 sheets of imperial cartridge drawing paper). Cut definite geometric shapes out of the collage, then use the shapes to build up a new design.

For sticking the pieces of paper or material onto the backing paper use a rubber solution (rubber cement) or spirit gum. Never use cold-water paste with paper as it makes the paper pulpy and difficult to manage. For tissue paper stick with white French polish or Cow gum (fig. 20).

21

Fig. 20 A cut paper collage

Textures

There are many ways of making textures for incorporation into designs, but it is not possible to list here more than a few. Some textures can also be used as designs in themselves.

Fig. 21 Drawings of brushwood in ink on wet paper

Coloured inks

Coloured inks washed over damp folded white paper give a delicate linear texture. The design can be carefully controlled if the paper is carefully folded before damping. Unfold the paper without completely flattening it. Carefully pour the ink, little by little, over the paper, which must be continually moved so that the ink runs into the creases and does not settle in a blot.

Before the paper is completely dry, stretch it by flattening it completely on a flat surface and sticking it down firmly round the edges with brown gummed paper. If the paper is allowed to dry without stretching it will be impossible to use in designing (fig. 21).

A different linear texture results from running lacquer paints over dry paper. Spread the paint quickly over one edge of the paper. By lifting the paper and moving it carefully it is possible to control the lines of paint.

Fig. 22 A stick printed pattern

Stick printing

One of the simplest and most inexpensive forms of pattern making is by using waste materials. There will be plenty of these in any home (fig. 22). Collect match boxes, cotton reels (spools), lids of varying sizes, corks, and so on. Make a pad of soft absorbent material, place in a saucer or suitable container and cover the pad with paint. Then use the articles that have been collected as though they were rubber stamps in a post office. For example, press the matchbox on to the paint pad and then on the paper. It is useful to try out as many objects as possible to see what sort of mark they make. Then select a few that make interesting marks and arrange them on the paper in a variety of patterns. Simple repetitive patterns can be made in this way, suitable for cotton prints.

24

Fig. 23 A repetitive potato pattern

Potato printing

Having experimented with objects that make a mark according to
their particular shape and size, try cutting simple patterns in
potatoes (fig. 23). First, cut the potato in half, to make a flat surface
on which to work. Then, using a pen knife or lino cutting tool,
gouge out lines or circles on the flat surface of the potato. Prepare
a paint pad, as described above, and press the potato on to it and
then onto the paper. Quite complicated patterns can be built up
by using more than one potato and more than one colour. If
preferred, the paint can be applied to the potato with a paint brush.
This takes longer than using a paint pad, but sometimes coats the
surface more evenly. Potatoes can also be cut into squares of
different sizes and printed to form mosaic patterns (fig. 24). Should
you wish to print the potato patterns directly onto the cloth, simply
spread fabric dye onto the pad instead of paint.

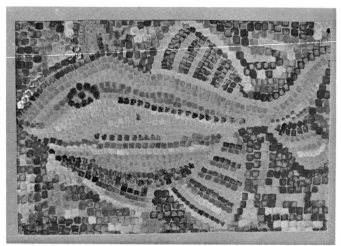
Fig. 24 A potato mosiac fish

Block printing

Potato patterns are limited by the size of the potato, so larger patterns can be obtained by cutting into wood or lino blocks (fig. 25). The principle remains the same in that the negative parts of the design are the areas that are cut away and will not print and the positive parts are the raised areas which will print. Lino blocks suitable for pattern cutting are obtainable from most art equipment shops. Wood blocks should be of soft wood, for example those which are easy to cut with simple tools.

Lino and wood blocks should be cut with special lino cutting or wood carving tools. These can be bought from suppliers of art and craft equipment. When printing lino blocks special printing inks must be used. Both oil bound and water bound printing inks are obtainable. Waterbound inks are recommended for use in the home as they are less messy and the equipment can be cleaned easily with water.

Fig. 25 A carved wooden block

Inking the lino block

A dye pad, as described for potato printing cannot be used for lino printing (fig. 26). The surface of lino (to which paint will not adhere), has to be coated with a printing ink. Put a teaspoonful of printing ink onto a sheet of glass, and with a photographic squeegee roller, roll the ink over the glass until it is of a 'tacky' consistency. Then transfer the ink to the lino block with the inked roller. Make certain that the paper to be printed is on a smooth surface which is well covered with newspaper. Then place the lino block on the paper and apply pressure to ensure an even print.

A wooden mallet can be used for this, but make certain that the face of the mallet falls squarely on to the block. Persian block printers in the bazaars hit the blocks with their fists which are padded with thick material. An even pressure can be achieved by using the floor as a base and standing on the blocks. Wood blocks can be printed either by using a dye pad or may be inked as described above (fig. 27).

Lino block and wood block printing provide excellent practice in 'repeating' a design (see page 45).

This practice will be invaluable when transferring designs onto screens.

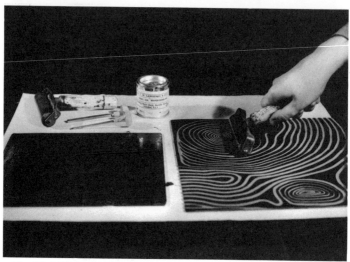

Fig. 26 Inking a lino block

Fig. 27 A print of the lino block

28

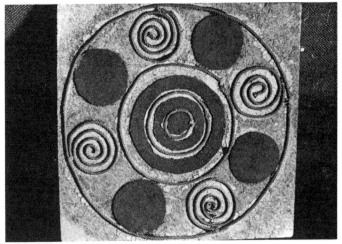

Fig. 28 A block showing the use of felt and string

String blocks and felt blocks

String and felt block patterns are made in exactly the reverse way from lino blocks and wood blocks. As has been said, with lino and wood the negative areas of the design are cut away leaving the raised areas to print. When using string and felt you glue the raised patterns or positive areas of the design onto the wood.

Interesting textured patterns can be made by using coarse string or rope. However, do not use string of different thicknesses on the same block. The raised printing surface must be level to ensure that all parts of the design will print. Provided the string used is soft and pliable it can be twisted into wavy lines and shapes, which are difficult to obtain when cutting a wood block. These string blocks are effective when overprinted on other designs. Use Evostik or Elmer's or any waterproof glue for sticking the string onto the block of wood (fig. 28).

When dry the block is ready for printing. The dye or paint can be applied with a large decorator's brush or by using a dye pad, large enough to hold the wood block (figs 29 and 30).

These four methods of block printing produce a tremendous variety of patterns and designs. Endless combinations can be obtained by overprinting and experimenting (fig. 31).

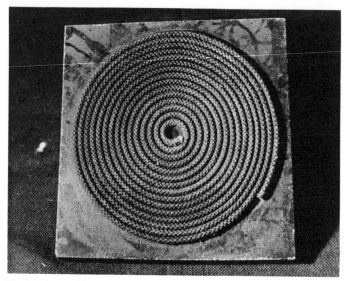

Fig. 29 A rope block

Wax crayon rubbings and drawings

The texture of wooden floors, manhole covers and types of frosted glass make interesting rubbings. Coloured wax crayons or a candle can be used. Place newsprint or thin cartridge (drawing) paper on top of the textured surface you have chosen, then rub as evenly as possible all over the surface of the paper. Be careful not to use the point of the crayon which might make holes in the paper (fig. 32, page 33).

Interesting colour effects can be obtained by washing dye or paint over the completed rubbing. As the wax crayon is greasy the dye does not take, leaving an interesting textured line. Wax crayons can be used for plant drawings and freehand pattern making, using the same technique of colour washing as above (fig. 34).

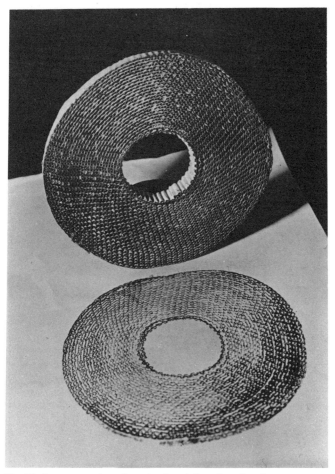

Fig. 30 A corrugated cardboard roll and the print taken from it

Fig. 31 A felt block

Drawing and painting on glass

Monotypes: A sheet of glass is inked with printing ink as described in the paragraph on lino blocks. Very little ink should be used, and it should be rolled until it is barely sticky. This is possible with printing inks as unlike poster paints, they are slow drying. Then place your paper onto the inked surface of the glass and draw on it with a pencil or pen. When the paper is removed from the glass it will be seen that a positive result has been obtained — the drawn lines will be black. If another sheet of paper is immediately smoothed onto the glass, without drawing on it, the result will be a negative print of the first drawing (figs 36, 37 and 38).

The same result can be achieved by scratching or drawing directly on the inked surface of the glass and taking off a paper print as before.

All the designs achieved by the above methods, i.e. stick printing, potato printing, block printing, string and felt printing, wax rubbings and drawings, monotypes, drawings and painting on glass, can be transferred onto screens and developed photographically as described in Chapter 6.

32

Fig. 32 Rubbings of coal hole covers

Fig. 34 Curtain fabric. The design developed from rubbings of coal hole covers

Opposite
Fig. 33 Wallhanging with screen-printed base and embroidered decoration

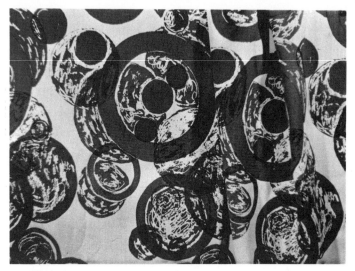

Fig. 35 A design based on wax circles

Starch paste patterns and drawings

Mix two dessertspoons of household starch into a thick paste with cold water. Then add boiling water stirring constantly until the mixture becomes a transparent bluey colour and is of a thick, creamy consistency. Now add powder paint or poster paint of the required colour to the starch paste and smooth the mixture over the paper. The starch paste takes approximately half an hour to dry. Using bits of cardboard, the backs of pencils or your fingers, draw into it leaving your pattern free of colour. If it dries while working, simply apply another coat of the paste.

Fig. 36 A monotype; drawing the positive

Fig. 37 Rubbing off the negative print

Fig. 38 Finished monotype drawings of corn showing the positive and negative

Bleach patterns and drawings

Cover a sheet of cartridge (drawing) paper with a coloured dye. Let it dry. Half fill a cup with ordinary household bleach, and by using pipe cleaners or sticks dipped in bleach, draw on the dyed paper. The bleach removes the dye, leaving the drawing white. Never use paint brushes in bleach because the bristles quickly rot.

Stick and potato printing, wood, felt and string blocks can be used for bleach printing if a small enamelled oven pan is used as a suitable container for the bleach. Lino blocks are not suitable for this process. Any bleach spilt on clothing must be washed off immediately with soap and water.

Fig. 39 A design of hair drawn and scratched directly onto glass

40

3 Screen preparation, table registration and printing

Fig. 40 Printed fabric showing a simple geometric repeat

Materials

Table
Padding
Table coverings
Table adhesives
    gum Arabic, Lankro,
    Sellotape (Scotch tape)
    or masking tape
Screen frames

Organdie
Staple gun, staples
Squeegees
Brown gummed paper
Fabric
Thin string
Tailor's chalk

It is necessary to cover the wooden frame of the screen with organdie. There are two simple methods by which this can be done. In both processes it is necessary to make sure that the warp and weft threads of the organdie run parallel to the side of the frame, otherwise fluting of the organdie will result and it will be impossible to stretch the cloth evenly. It is not possible to print with a screen if the organdie has been distorted while stretching it over the frame (fig. 41).

Stapling method: For this process it is necessary to obtain a staple gun. Using the selvedge of the organdie as a guide, staple two sides of the material on to sides 1 and 2 of the screen. Any stretching or pulling must be avoided. The staples must be placed as close together as possible.

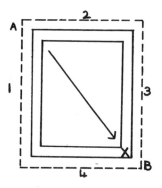

Fig. 41 Covering a screen

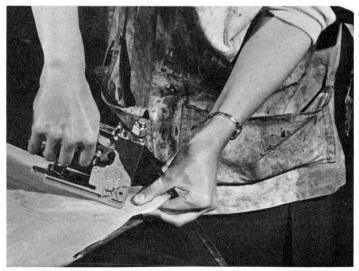

Fig. 42 Stretching the diagonal corner

Then stretch the organdie diagonally from A to B (fig. 42), securing it at point x. This ensures that the warp and weft threads of the organdie are parallel with the screen frame. Then, stretching evenly and firmly, staple the opposite sides of the frame, first side 3 and then 4, until the organdie is perfectly smooth and· taut (fig. 43). After covering a screen by this method, it is advisable to coat the stapled surfaces with shellac, not only for extra strength, but to prevent the organdie from tearing (fig. 44).

Shellac method: This method of covering a frame takes slightly longer than the stapling method, but is perfectly satisfactory if no staple gun is obtainable. Coat sides 1 and 2 of the screen frame with shellac. Allow the shellac to become tacky. Then, using the selvedge of the organdie as a guide, carefully smooth two sides of the material on to the sides of the screen frame which have been covered with shellac. Once again, avoid stretching or pulling as this will distort the organdie. Wait until sides 1 and 2 are thoroughly dry and then follow the same stretching procedure as explained in the stapling method.

The prepared screen is now ready for use in any one of the ways described in further chapters, but it will require further treatment if the photographic method is used, as described in Chapter 6.

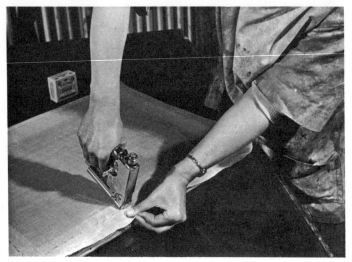

Fig. 43 Stretching the opposite side

Fig. 44 Coating the screen frame with shellac

Putting a design into repeat

Whenever a screen is not being used simply for picture-making or for articles such as table mats, cushion covers and tea towels which do not require a repeating pattern, the problem of 'putting the design into repeat' arises. When designing for dress lengths or curtains, the pattern has to be repeated many times during printing. Therefore, if the design does not repeat accurately, bad joins can ruin the finished print. 'Putting a design into repeat' is rather like cutting out a jig-saw puzzle.

First, it is necessary to establish the size of the repeat, which is determined by the width of the fabric to be printed.

Furnishing fabrics are normally 48″ wide and dress fabrics normally 36″ wide. Therefore the width of the repeat can be any multiple of 48″ or 36″, as the case may be (figs 45 to 50). The

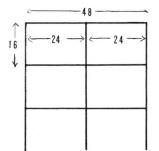

Fig. 45 12″×12″ repeat for 48″ fabric

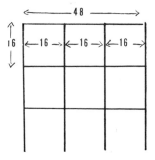

Fig. 46 16″ × 16″ repeat for 48″ fabric

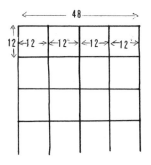

Fig. 47 24″ × 16″ repeat for 48″ fabric

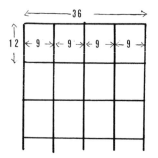

Fig. 48 9" × 12" repeat for 36"
fabric

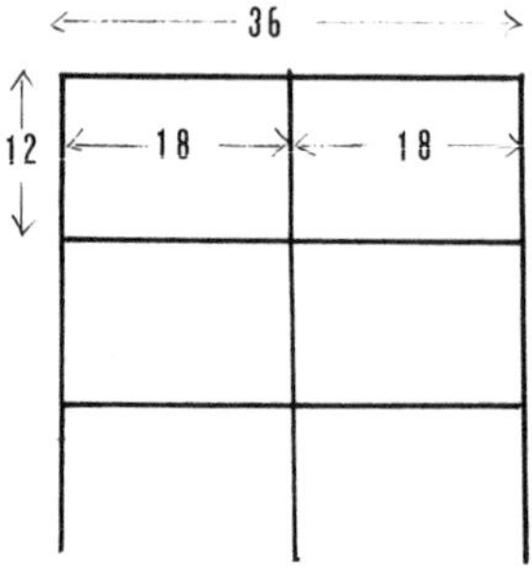

Fig. 49 18" × 12" repeat for 36"
fabric

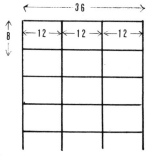

Fig. 50 12" × 18" repeat for 36"
fabric

height of the repeat will depend on the length of fabric you are printing or on the size of your screen.

Having decided on the size of the repeat, rule the registration lines accurately around the design, always extending the lines to form crosses (fig. 51). These will help with the registration of the design on the cloth. Sometimes the design fits perfectly within the registration lines (fig. 52), but sometimes it overlaps the lines and becomes like a jig-saw puzzle, each side having to fit into the other (fig. 53).

Wherever the design overlaps line A, it has to overlap line B and similarly lines C and D. The only way this can be done accurately is to trace the design using the crosses of the repeat lines as registration marks (fig. 53). Then move the tracing paper from line A to B and C to D, making sure that the design fits on all sides.

46

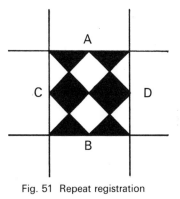

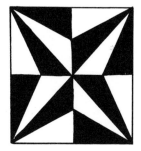

Fig. 51 Repeat registration

Fig. 52 Design fitting within the repeat lines

Half drop repeats: Very often, expecially with floral designs, a 'half drop repeat' is more suitable than a 'side by side repeat'. Printing a design with a half-drop repeat requires a more complicated table-registration. Depending on the width of the design, register the table with two, three or four columns of equal width (figs 54 and 55).

Fig. 53 A jig-saw puzzle repeat

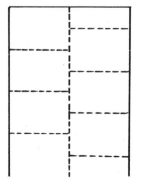

Fig. 54 Table registration for a half-drop repeat

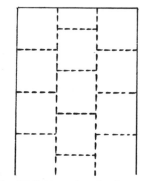

Fig. 55 Table registration for a half-drop repeat

Starting from one end and working down the length of the material register each alternate column with the depth of the design. With the remaining column or columns, the registration does not begin at the top edge of the material, but half way down the first repeat of the adjacent columns.

When printing the design it is therefore necessary to print down alternate columns leaving every other print clear in the usual way (figs 56 and 57).

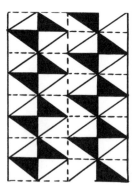

Fig. 56 A printed geometric half-drop design

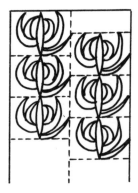

Fig. 57 A printed floral half-drop design

Fig. 58 Tracing a design onto the screen

Transferring the design onto the screen

The design is now ready to be transferred onto the screen. Place the screen on top of the design with the outside surface face down, and, with a soft pencil, trace the design onto the organdie (fig.58). Then turn the screen over and, on the outside surface, paint with shellac all the areas of the design not to be printed (fig. 59). Therefore, the clear area will then print. This is the simplest method of preparing a screen for printing. In order to avoid 'pinholes', it is necessary to give it at least two coats of shellac.

Further and more complicated methods of transferring a design onto a screen are described in Chapter 6.

Fig. 59 Painting the screen with shellac

Registration of fabric

Methods of fixing the fabric to the printing table:

1 When printing very thin fabric, such as muslin or terylene (polyester) net, it is necessary to cover the printing table with unbleached calico. This serves as a backcloth, soaking up the absorbent dye which floods through the muslin when printing. Then pin the muslin onto the backcloth using the selvedge as a guide. Always keep the selvedge parallel with the edge of the table. Then gently stretch the cloth across the table and pin down the opposite selvedge. All distortion of the threads must be avoided. Finally, pin the top of the fabric and stretching the cloth lengthwise, secure the bottom. The pinned sides can be covered with Sellotape (Scotch tape), so that the pins will not damage the screen.

2 If the printing table has a waterproof or rubber type covering, and you are not using a fine fabric, the surface of the table is coated with gum Arabic.

The best way of coating the table with gum Arabic is to smooth it on with a squeegee in exactly the same way as when dye is pulled through a screen. Allow the gum to dry thoroughly. Then iron the fabric onto the gummed table, keeping the warp and weft threads parallel to the edges. It is important for the fabric to be

Fig. 60 Wallpaper printed with a shellac screen

Fig. 61 Bathmat printed with a shellac screen

Fig. 62 Table registration

absolutely smooth. Any creases or wrinkles will affect the finished product. The gum Arabic coating will only last for one printing. After the printed fabric has been removed, the table should be thoroughly washed with soap and water.

3 A semi-permanent table adhesive called 'Lankro', used for sticking the fabric to the table, is available in Great Britain and is recommended if a lot of printing is to be done. This is applied in the same way as gum Arabic but with this method no ironing is required. The fabric is simply smoothed on and the surface of the table remains sticky for about six printings. After using Lankro, it is necessary to clean the squeegee and table with turps substitute.

4 If no gum Arabic or Lankro are available (as in the US for example), Sellotape (Scotch tape) or masking tape can be used. The fabric is fixed to the table in the same way as described in (1).

Table registration

Mark out the repeat size of the design along the length and breadth of the fabric. The marking of the fabric requires two people. Thin

Fig. 63 Registering the paper design

string is rubbed with tailors' chalk before it is stretched across the fabric from point A to B (fig. 62). By lifting the taut string and letting it spring back onto the cloth the chalked string will leave a mark. This chalk mark is not permanent and can be rubbed off.

Screen registration

1 Place the paper design on the fabric so that the crosses of the repeat lines coincide with the crosses of the chalk lines on the fabric (fig. 63).
2 Place the screen on top of the design so that it fits exactly (fig. 64).
3 With a felt pen mark the outside of the screen frame wherever it touches the registration lines on the cloth. This will be in eight places (fig. 65).

It is most important to follow these steps exactly and to register the screen as accurately as possible. These registration marks will ensure that the screen is not misplaced when printing.

Fig. 64 Placing the screen on top of the design

Fig. 65 The frame marked where
it meets the registration lines

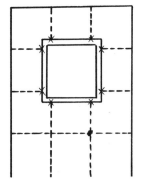

Printing method

Again it is necessary for two people to carry out this process unless
the screens are very small. Before starting to print, mask the screen
with gummed brown paper strips, up to the edge of the design.
Always do a trial print on paper first in order to discover whether
the screen has 'pinholes' and in order to wet the screen through
thoroughly. Then, placing the screen onto the cloth so that the
registration marks fit with those on the cloth, proceed with

Fig. 66 Printing the fabric

Fig. 67 Printing alternate repeats

Fig. 68 The finished fabric

printing. Place the dye in the dye-well (see page 98), at one side of the screen. While one person holds the screen firmly in position, the other pulls the dye across the screen with a squeegee. One pull should be sufficient for a very thin fabric, such as net, but it should be pulled through twice for all other materials except very thick ones such as hessian (burlap) or towelling, which need three or four pulls to make sure that the dye penetrates the cloth. When printing a length, print every alternate repeat so as to avoid the screen being put down on wet dye (figs 66 to 68).

Fixing of printed fabric

The dyes recommended in this book are all 'fixed' by ironing, so no complicated equipment is needed. The completed fabric should first be hung up for about twenty-four hours to dry thoroughly

Fig. 69 Washing a screen

and then ironed very slowly, first on the wrong side and then on the right side. A strong smell is given off when ironing. This is caused by the chemical reaction in the dye stuff and the smell is not lasting or in any way harmful.

After fixing, the fabrics are washable, but they should not be boiled.

Washing screens

It is important to remember to wash the screens thoroughly immediately after use. If they are left to dry while still full of dye, they will clog and be unusable in the future. If properly looked after, a well-made screen should last for printing at least twenty yards of fabric before becoming worn (fig. 69).

4 Experimental screens

Fig. 70 Draped fabric based on a textured wax design

Materials

Squeegee
Screen frames and organdie
Household dye
Decorator's brush and
    paint brushes (assorted)
Lace or open weave fabric
Printing dyes
Natural objects e.g. leaves
    feathers
    string
    raffia etc.

Paper – for prints and
    for tearing
Candle
Black wax crayon
Newspapers
Rags
Brown gummed paper
Paper doyleys
Shellac
Tusche (lithographic ink)
Rex cold water paste
    (wallpaper paste)
Household bleach

To gain experience in handling screens and in pattern making, experimental screens are invaluable. The patterns evolved by these methods are not intended as designs in themselves but as experiments to be used later with other more permanent methods of printing. None of these designs are for immediate transference on to material. White or dye-washed paper is easy, quick and cheap to use, and therefore very suitable for this experimental work.

Dye-washing

Dye: use Dylon (Tintex) or any household dye. Mix the dye with water to its normal consistency and wash onto the paper with a large, soft, decorator's brush.

Textured screens

One of the easiest ways of experimenting with texture and simple pattern is to cover the screen with an open-weave material instead of organdie. Any kind of loosely constructed meshed material will do. The simplest to use are net curtaining or lace. The screen should be covered with the material in the way already described in the preceding chapter. Stretch the material as tightly as possible, without distorting the weave (fig. 71).

Thick flowing dyes are the best to use with these open-work screens, as they are stiffer and less likely to blur the textures by flooding underneath the mesh.

Having covered the screen, pull the dye through onto the

Fig. 71 Screen covered with lace

Fig. 72 Pouring dye into the dye-well

Fig. 73 Pulling dye across the screen

Fig. 74 Pulling dye across the screen

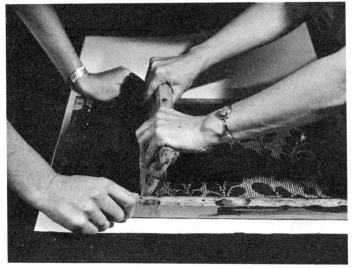

61

Fig. 75 The finished print (a) 1 pull of the squeegee (b) 2 pulls of the squeegee

paper with a squeegee, as you would with an organdie screen. More unusual patterns occur when you overprint, placing the same screen at a different angle with each subsequent print (figs 72 to 75).

The use of natural objects

These can be used with an organdie covered screen. Interesting decorative effects can be obtained by using flowers, leaves, feathers, grasses, strands of wool or string (fig. 76).
When using flowers or leaves it is advisable to press them first as flat as possible. When the flower or leaf is too lumpy the print will be blurred because the screen will not be pressed flat enough onto the printing surface. Also avoid holly leaves or prickly plants, as these will tear the organdie.

Arrange the objects on the printing paper, firmly placing the screen on top of them. The pressure of the screen will keep them in position while the dye is pulled through with the squeegee (figs 77 to 79).

Fig. 76 Leaves arranged on the paper

Fig. 77 Covering the leaves with the screen

63

Fig. 78 Lifting the screen after printing

Fig. 79 Finished print

Waxed screen

There are two methods of waxing a screen, either to gain a texture or to evolve a simple pattern. In both cases an organdie screen is needed.

For the first process, rub an ordinary white candle or black wax crayon over the outer surface of the organdie. By occasionally holding the screen up to the light you will be able to follow the pattern you are drawing (fig. 80). The subtle textures formed by the wax can be used as designs in themselves, or incorporated into a larger design (fig. 81).

The second method requires a shallow metal trough and a constant low heat. Instead of using the candle as a solid block, melt it in the trough over a low heat and keep the wax in a liquid state all the time you need to use it.

Place the screen on several sheets of newspaper with the outer surface of the organdie upwards. Dip a paint brush into the liquid wax and paint your design onto the screen surface. As the wax soon dries on the organdie, it is necessary to work fairly quickly.

Never use the wax on the inside of the screen because the action of the squeegee will crack and smudge the wax.

Fig. 80 A waxed screen ready to print

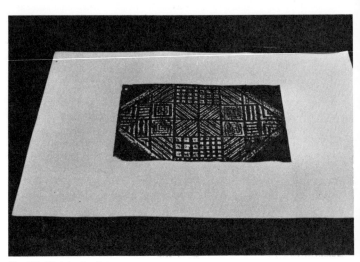

Fig. 81 Finished print

Paper stencils—organdie screens

Stencils can be cut or torn from any fairly strong paper, for example, newsprint or cartridge (drawing) paper. Using a sheet of paper large enough to cover the outer surface of the screen, cut or tear out a pattern of any size to fit within the screen. If the stencil is cut out of cartridge paper, stick it onto the outside surface of the screen with adhesive tape. If newsprint is used it is not necessary to stick the stencil to the screen. As the newsprint is lighter than cartridge paper it will adhere to the screen after the first print (figs 82 and 83).

When cutting the stencil, it is advisable to keep the areas of paper fairly broad, as the dye weakens it and causes it to tear easily. It is also possible to use ready-made stencils, such as paper doyleys in exactly the same way (figs 84 and 85).

The negative form of stencilling can also provide effective patterns. Simply tear or cut out complete shapes and arrange them on the printing paper. Place the screen on top of them allowing the pressure of the screen to hold them in place and pull the dye through (figs 88 to 91).

Fig. 82 A cut paper stencil positive

Fig. 83 A cut paper stencil negative

Fig. 84 Paper doyleys for use as stencils

Fig. 85 Finished print of doyleys

Fig. 86 Two-coloured print based on cog wheels

Fig. 87 Four-colour wallpaper

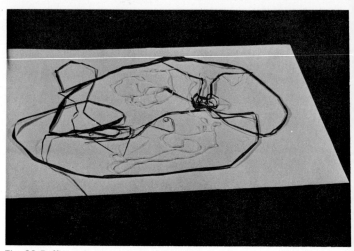

Fig. 88 Raffia and string arranged on paper

Fig. 89 The screen being lifted off the print showing the string adhering to screen

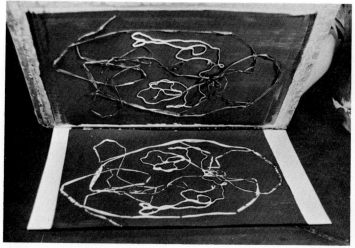

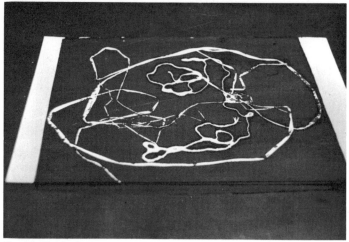

Fig. 90 Finished print

Shellac screens
The solvent for shellac is methylated spirits — alcohol

This is a development of the paper stencil method. Instead of using paper shapes to mask the screen the design is painted onto the outside surface with shellac. With this medium it is possible to achieve fairly detailed designs.

Shellac is quick drying, but two coats are necessary to make sure that the masked parts of the screen have no 'pinholes' where the dye could seep through when printing. As soon as the shellac is dry, the screen is ready for use and will last a considerable time, unlike the paper stencil which will become saturated with dye fairly quickly and disintegrate. The screens should be washed in lukewarm water as very hot water softens shellac.

Unlike any of the other experimental methods, shellac screens can be used for a repeat pattern on fabric if required (see figs 60 and 61).

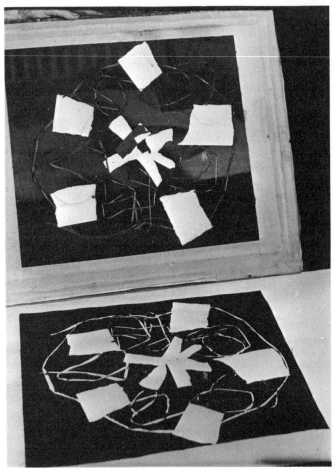

Fig. 91 Combination of torn paper shapes and raffia

Fig. 92 Painting a Tusche screen

Tusche screens

Tusche is a lithographic ink obtainable from: T. N. Lawrence and Son, Bleeding Heart Yard, London, E.C.1, or can be mixed by a chemist according to the following recipe:

    30 grms lamp black
  200 grms gum tragacanth
  100 ccs olive oil
  620 ccs sodium silicate 90° plus 10
(made up to 1 litre – a little less than a quart)

Using the Tusche mixture paint the design onto the outside surface of the screen. When the Tusche is dry cover the entire outside surface of the screen, including the Tusche, with shellac. The shellac will not penetrate the area covered by the Tusche because of its oily quality (fig. 92).

After the shellac has dried, the screen is washed on both sides with warm water. This will dissolve the Tusche, leaving the pattern clear and ready to print.

If a design with fine lines is required, a Tusche pencil should be used as the liquid Tusche is only suitable for bold designs. Similar effects to wax rubbings will be formed by the shellac penetrating the Tusche where it has been more thinly applied.

Bleach paste

Paste: Rex cold water paste or any wallpaper paste.

Mix the paste, using bleach or a blend of water and bleach, to a medium consistency. Always add the powdered paste to the liquid, never add the liquid to the powder. The consistency of the paste should be thick enough to move easily across the screen when pulled with the squeegee. If it is too thin it will flood under the screen. Do not leave the paste standing too long or it will break down under the action of the bleach and become completely liquid. If this should happen, more powder can be added to the liquid, but this weakens the action of the bleach. So always experiment with the paste before using it on the design.

The use of bleach in design acts as a negative form of printing. Instead of building up colour in layers, the design is created by the action of the bleach on dye washed paper. The colour disappears in the areas which are touched by the bleach paste. The colour of the bleached areas varies according to the strength of the paste. When the paste is mixed entirely with bleach the dye disappears completely, leaving a white area. But if varying amounts of water are mixed with the paste, the bleach is weakened and some of the dye colour remains. The bleached areas are then only a paler shade of the main dye colour.

Bleach paste can be used on paper with any of the experimental screen methods. But never use it on fabric as the bleach rots the fibres.

5 Profilm screens

Fig. 93 Fabric printed with a Profilm screen

Fig. 94 Ironing on Profilm

Materials

Cutting knives
Soft pencils
Profilm
Ironing blanket and cloth
Iron (not steam)

Brown gummed paper
Copal varnish
French polish (shellac)
Printing paper

Profilm screens are the next natural step from shellac screens. Designs printed by the Profilm method are precise and clear-edged. It is possible to achieve more definition of detail in designing and Profilm screens last for a longer time than those made with shellac.

The process of designing and printing with profilm is that of the true stencil. The shapes cut out of the Profilm are the areas where the dye will come through onto the material.

Profilm itself is a layer of wax with a greaseproof paper backing. As it is semi-transparent it is possible to lay it over the previously prepared design and follow the lines through it.

Fig. 95 Stripping off the greaseproof paper backing

For cutting the Profilm, you will need a flat surface on which to lay both the design and Profilm. Because of the nature of the Profilm it is not possible to reproduce heavily textured designs. This process is for clear-edged designs and large areas of flat colour. The amount of fine detail it is possible to produce depends entirely on your capability in cutting the Profilm precisely. It is therefore sensible to start with relatively simple designs until you are used to handling the cutting scalpel.

When you have decided on the design you wish to use, draw out the repeat of the design carefully on firm white drawing paper (cartridge paper) and paint in the colours you want to use onto the design. When finished, the paper designs should be an exact coloured replica of one repeat of the design.

Pin the paper design firmly to a flat surface and cut a piece of Profilm to cover the design, leaving about two inches of Profilm spare around the edges.

With the shiny wax side of the Profilm upwards, lay it over the design, making sure that both the design and the Profilm are absolutely flat. Pin the Profilm firmly at each corner, making sure that it is not possible for it to slip during the cutting process. A

Fig. 96 Masking the screen with brown gummed paper

separate stencil must be prepared for each colour in the design. For example, if the design contains three colours, three stencils must be cut and three screens made, one to hold each stencil.

Having decided which colour the particular stencil is for, cut carefully round each area of the colour. When cutting it is important to avoid cutting through the greaseproof backing of the Profilm as this holds the stencil together until it is transferred to the screen. It is therefore wise to experiment first with a small piece of Profilm to test the pressure needed to cut the wax layer cleanly and leave the backing paper intact.

As each area of colour is completed, carefully peel off each piece of Profilm contained within the cut area. When each area containing a particular colour has been cut and peeled off, unpin the Profilm stencil and make a note on the edge of the colour it represents.

When you have completed each stencil for each colour, prepare the appropriate number of screens. Each screen must, of course, be big enough to contain the whole repeat and leave about

78

Fig. 97 Masking the screen with brown gummed paper

four inches at either end, for the dye-wells. The screens should be prepared to the extent of the first layer of gummed brown paper around the edges.

Cover a table or flat working surface (big enough to hold the screen easily), with a thick blanket. Cover this with a piece of smooth material, for example, an old sheet.

To fix the Profilm onto the screen, it is necessary to iron it on with a medium to cool iron—not steam (fig. 94).

Place the Profilm with its shiny wax side up, again making sure that it is absolutely flat. The screen must then be placed over it with the outside surface of the screen lying flat on the Profilm. Then iron gently all over the inside surface of the screen.

It takes a few minutes of gentle ironing to melt the wax sufficiently to transfer it to the screen. When the wax turns darker over the complete area of the Profilm, stop ironing and turn the screen over. If the wax has been properly ironed onto the screen, the greaseproof paper backing should be completely mottled with white. This is where the backing paper is already beginning to

Fig. 98 The screen ready for printing

peel away from the wax. If the backing is not completely mottled, continue ironing the inside of the screen, checking the backing continually. When the ironing is completed, turn the screen over so that the outside surface of the screen is uppermost.

The next process of stripping off the greaseproof paper backing must be carried through very carefully. It is easier to start at an outside corner of the Profilm and gently separate the backing from the wax. Loosen it for about three inches either way from the corner and gently pull diagonally across the Profilm. If there is any resistance from the wax, stop, and tear off the areas that have been separated; although, if the Profilm has been properly ironed, the paper should strip off fairly easily. If it is difficult to strip any area, iron it again, taking care not to touch any area that is already stripped otherwise the wax will melt and come off onto the sheet covering the table.

To fix the Profilm permanently to the screen and to make it waterproof, complete the gummed brown paper strapping at the ends and sides of the screen, and just cover the edges of the

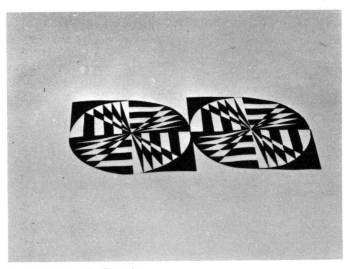

Fig. 99 Finished Profilm print

Profilm (figs 96 and 97).

Profilm is available in America from screen suppliers. Also commonly used in America is amber film. The process is the same, using amber film, except that the film is secured to the screen with an application of an adhering fluid rather than by ironing.

The final step in the preparation of the screen is to coat the inside surface with Copal varnish. Paint only small areas at a time, covering the Profilm, the plain organdie and the gummed brown paper. With a soft cloth soaked in turpentine or turps. substitute, rub the screen from the outside, making sure that the areas not covered with Profilm are clear of varnish. This ensures waterproofing and strengthens the fibres of the organdie so that the screen can be washed any number of times without damage.

When the Copal varnish is completely dry, paint white French polish or shellac on the outside of the screen and rub on the inside with methylated spirits (alcohol). When the French polish or shellac is completely dry, the screens are ready for printing (figs 98 and 99).

81

6 Photographic screens

Fig. 100 Single-coloured photographic screen print

Equipment and materials

Table large enough to hold screen.

One sheet of glass large enough to completely cover the screen.

A board and old blanket for padding the inside of the screen.

500 watt lamp or bulb.

Red or Yellow safe bulb.

Gelatine and potassium dichromate.

Black cellulose lacquer (UK), screen block-out lacquer (USA).

Gas ring or hot plate.

Four-inch sash brush.

Cupboard large enough to hold screen (lightproof).

Bath or sink and hose pipe.

Kodatrace.

Photopake.

Copal varnish.

Coating the screen

1 The screen is covered in the usual way.

2 Prepare the gelatine according to the recipe:

Recipe for 10% solution

      10 grms gelatine   *or* 4 dessertspoons gelatine

      90 ccs water   1 pt. of water

3 Use a double boiler, and always mix the gelatine with cold water. Sprinkle it into the water and heat; allow to dissolve. Do not stir, as vigorous stirring will make the mixture frothy and these bubbles, if applied to the screen, will burst and form 'pinholes' when dry. Heat the gelatine to blood temperature and do *not* allow it to boil for the same reasons given above. Should froth form on the top of the mixture, remove it with newspaper or blotting paper before coating the screen.

4 Apply three coats of gelatine onto the outside surface of the screen as smoothly as possible. This is best done by sweeping the four-inch brush across the screen in firm movements. Each brush-load of gelatine should overlap the other slightly, to avoid gaps. Apply each coating of gelatine in opposite directions, allowing each one to dry thoroughly before applying the next (figs 101 and 102).

For example: 1st coat A to B

             2nd coat C to D

             3rd coat A to B

This will make a really strong screen and ensure that every part of the screen has been properly covered. Gelatine is colourless, so when coating the screen put a chalk arrow and a number on

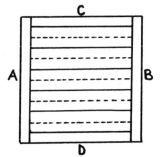

Fig. 101 Diagrams of coating the screen with gelatine

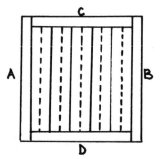

Fig. 102 Diagrams of coating the screen

the wooden frame to show in which direction the gelatine has been applied, and how many coats have been given. Keep the gelatine on a low heat and do not allow it to get cool while in use or the mixture will not flow evenly onto the screen.

5 The screen is now ready for either the daylight method or the darkroom method of developing.

Daylight developing

1 Gelatine is semi-transparent, so once again, as with the shellac screen described in Chapter 3, place the screen onto the design, with the outside surface face down and trace through with a soft pencil.

2 The design is then painted onto the outside surface of the screen with black cellulose lacquer (screen block-out lacquer) or any quick-drying household enamel paint. The important thing is that the medium used should not be soluble in water. Notice that, unlike the shellac screens, (Chapter 3) the lacquer is applied to the *positive* parts of the design, i.e. the parts which *are* to be printed.

3 A detailed design with fine lines is not suitable as the lacquer must be applied thickly. Check for 'pinholes' by holding the screen up to the light. Give an extra coat of lacquer where necessary.

4 When the lacquer is completely dry, a solution of potassium dichromate is painted over the entire outside surface of the

screen. The potassium solution will not penetrate the lacquer, provided there are no 'pinholes' in it.

5 Then leave the screen in the daylight until the potassium (which is bright yellow when applied), is dry and has turned a golden-brown colour. The screen should always be left to dry in a horizontal position. The length of time needed for the potassium to change colour depends on the strength of the daylight (two to four hours is normal). Potassium dichromate is sensitive to light, and therefore, when exposed, hardens those parts of the screen that have not been protected by the lacquer.

6 Then wash the screen with hot water (not boiling), by hosing the inside of the screen. Never hose on the outside surface, this will dislodge the gelatine film, weaken the screen and blur the edges of the design. The action of hosing with hot water causes the gelatine underneath the lacquered parts to swell and forces the lacquer up so that it can be peeled off, leaving the design clear. The water does not penetrate the potassiumed parts of the screen, which have hardened in the light and become water-proof. Having removed all the lacquer, give the clear areas of the design another hosing to make sure that they are not still clogged with gelatine. Finally, hose with cold water, and leave the screen lying flat to dry.

7 To strengthen the screen before printing, apply a coat of clear varnish (Copal) to the inside of the screen, using a soft, decorator's brush, and rub with a soft, absorbent cloth on the outside surface to make sure the clear areas of the design remain clear. It is advisable to varnish small areas at a time. If any varnish remains in the clear areas, rub with a cloth that has been damped with turpentine substitute.

8 Finally cover the outside surface of the screen, up to the edges of the design, with brown gummed paper in the usual way and the screen is ready for printing. These screens are strong and will last a long time.

Dark room process
General procedure

The covered screen is painted with a sensitising solution and is dried in the dark. The pattern to be produced is painted on transparent paper with a dense opaque ink. This painted pattern is known as the positive. A separate positive and screen are necessary for each colour of the design. The positive is now placed in contact with the sensitised screen and exposed to light. The length of exposure varies according to the actual distance from the source of light and the type of light used. The exposed screen is now well washed, first in cold water to harden the negative parts of the design and then in hot water to remove the soluble gelatine which has been protected by the positive. Allow the screen to dry slowly then strengthen it with a coat of varnish before printing.

Sensitising the screen

Recipe	*or*
1 pt. water	1 pt. water
2 oz. gelatine	4 level dessertspoons of gelatine
$\frac{1}{2}$ oz. potassium dichromate	1 level dessertspoon of potassium dichromate.

2 The screen can be coated with the sensitising solution in daylight, but must be dried in the dark, a light-proof cupboard being the most satisfactory. After coating and drying, it should only be examined in a safe light. It should not be left in the dark cupboard for more than twenty-four hours or decomposition of the sensitising solution will occur.

Preparing the positive design

By the time the screen has been coated and placed in the dark cupboard the design should already have been put into repeat. Each of the colours of the design are now traced and painted onto separate sheets of transparent tracing paper Kodatrace (frosted acetate). The design must be painted onto the matt surface of the Kodatrace (frosted acetate) with opaque ink. Photopake (negative photo opaque) or Astropake (fig. 106). It is essential that the positive really is opaque or light will penetrate it and spoil the design.

Transferring the 'positive' design to the organdie screen

1 Take the screen from the dark cupboard and prepare it for developing. At this stage, always work under the red or yellow safe light (fig. 107).
2 To ensure good contact between the positive and the organdie,

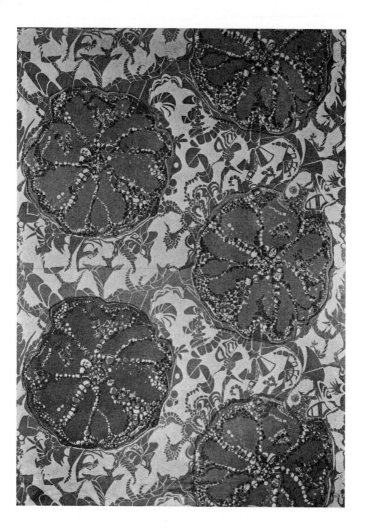

Fig. 103 Two-coloured photographic screen print

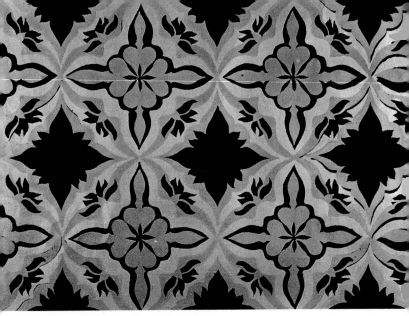

Fig. 104 Screen printed wall paper

Fig. 105 Screen printed bath towel

Fig. 106 Painting a Kodatrace

the hollow underside of the screen should be supported by a padded wooden block which just fits inside it.

3 The positive is now laid flat on the dry sensitized organdie, covered with a sheet of glass and weighted on the four corners. The positive must be flat and in close contact with the organdie or the design will have blurred edges (fig. 108).

4 The screen is now ready for developing. The light should be 18" above the screen, but lengths of exposure vary according to the strength of the light used and conditions, and although a table of suggested times is given, these would have to be tried until the most suitable time for particular conditions has been found (fig. 109).

5 After exposure, remove the glass and the positive. The screen is washed immediately, first in cold water to set the gelatine and the potassium surrounding the design, and then in hot water to dissolve the soluble gelatine, which has been protected by the opaque substance painted on your positive. Wash the screen thoroughly, so as to remove all the gelatine from the clear parts of the design.

Fig. 107 Preparing the pad for developing

Always remember to wash the screen on the inside so as not to dislodge the gelatine film on the outside surface and blur the design.

6 When dry, the screen is coated with varnish (see page 83) for extra strength.

Fig. 108 The padded screen with Kodatrace

Suggested times of exposure of screen

Exposure of the screen can be carried out in daylight, but accurate timing will have to be established by trial and error.

Daylight exposure	Distance from light source	Time of exposure required
Strong sunlight		5 mins
Bright daylight		10 mins
Dull daylight		up to 2 hrs
Darkroom exposure		
40 watt fluorescent lamps (placed one to every 6″ of screen)	8″	2 to 5 mins
150 watt lamp	18″	3 hrs
300 watt lamp	24″	up to 2 hrs
500 watt lamp	18″	5 to 10 mins

Fig. 109 Screen and Kodatrace under glass ready for developing

Possible sources of trouble in screen making

A Pinholes in the gelatine and potassium dichromate film.
Cause:
    1 Frothing of the sensitizing solution.
    2 Uneven application of the sensitizing solution.
    3 The sensitizing solution incompletely mixed.
    4 Dust on the screen before coating.

B Exposed gelatine film is partly or completely washed out.
Cause:
    1 Under-exposed.
    2 Sensitizing solution heated to too high a temperature causing decomposition.
    3 Very humid atmospheric conditions during application of sensitizing solution.

Fig. 110 Peacock feathers being developed

C Gelatine and potassium dichromate coating *not* completely removed from clear areas of the design.
Cause:
1 Over-exposed.
2 Temperature too high during exposure.
3 Screens kept too long at a high temperature before exposure.
4 The positive not completely opaque.

D The designs have poor edges and the lines have closed up in places.
Cause:
1 The screen has not been in perfect contact with the positive.
2 The coating is too thick.

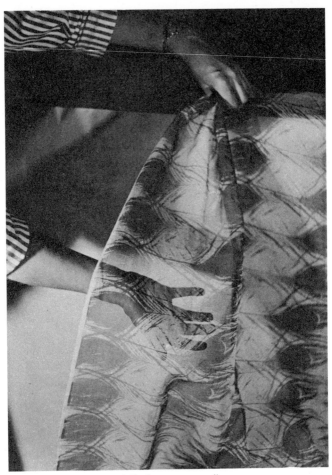

Fig. 111 Print of peacock feathers on organdie

Experimental photographic developing

Various media can be used as alternatives to Kodatrace (frosted acetate) positives, which can give most exciting and lasting results. The methods described on pages 59 to 71 in Chapter 4 probably produced some very interesting patterns and designs, but at that stage they were still experimental. Now having mastered 'repeats' and the photographic developing of screens, it will be possible to use, in a more permanent way, the designs obtained experimentally in Chapter 4.

Instead of Kodatrace (frosted acetate) painted with an opaque ink, the positive now becomes any one of the materials or objects described in Chapter 4:

1 Net curtaining
2 Lace
3 Crocheted doyleys
4 Paper doyleys
5 Cut paper stencils
6 Feathers
7 Grasses
8 Strands of wool or string.

These can be laid directly onto the sensitised surface of the screen (fig. 110), covered with a sheet of glass to ensure good contact with the organdie and exposed in the normal way. When the screen is washed it will be seen that the object, the doyley, for example, has in fact taken the place of the opaque ink (positive) and prevented the light from passing through it. The gelatine underneath it will remain soluble and wash out, leaving the clear pattern of the doyley permanently on the screen. It is important to see that all objects placed on the screen in this way are really opaque, or the light will pass through them and the design will not be clear.

Oiled paper positives

Newsprint (unprinted newspaper) or thin tracing paper can be used to make successful oiled paper positives. Wax rubbings of wood, manhole covers, and a great variety of textures can be made on the newsprint. A black wax crayon applied as thickly as possible should be used for these rubbings.

Other patterns can be painted onto the newsprint using black poster paint or ink. Always use black as this ensures that the positive is opaque. Then oil the back of the newsprint with olive oil or liquid paraffin, rubbing it well into the paper with the palm of the hand (fig. 112). The oil makes the newsprint sufficiently transparent to allow the light to pass through it and the black waxed or painted areas become the positive (fig. 113).

Direct painting on glass

Any design can be painted directly onto a sheet of glass. Black poster paint is recommended so that the positive is thoroughly opaque. Both oiled paper 'positives' and 'glass positives' are developed in the usual way. The oiled paper and the glass are a substitute for Kodatrace (frosted acetate). The black paint or wax take the place of the Photopake or opaque substance used in painting the design (see fig. 39).

If each step of the developing procedure is closely followed, the screen should be able to print at least twenty yards of fabric before showing signs of wear.

Fig. 112 Oiling a newsprint positive based on a lino block (see fig. 26)

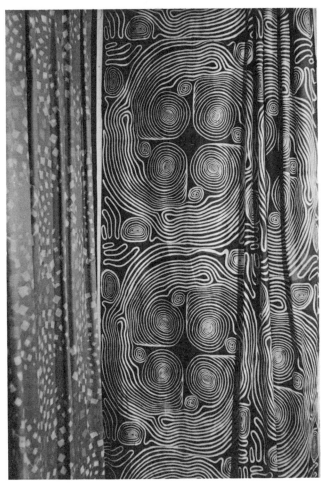

Fig. 113 Finished curtain length

Definitions of trade terms

Putting a design into repeat: A phrase used to describe the way in which a design is measured and joined before printing a length of fabric.

Kodatrace (frosted acetate): A transparent photographic film used when transferring designs onto screens (see Chapter 6).

Photopake (negative photo opaque): This is an opaque ink used for painting the positive areas of the design onto Kodatrace (see Chapter 6).
Opaque ink is sold under various trade names, for example, Photographic Opaque, Astropake etc.

Pinholes: When coating the screen with shellac or gelatine, air bubbles often cause small holes. These are referred to as pinholes.

Dye-wells: Dye-wells are the spaces that are left between the design and the screen frame for holding the dye (fig. 72).

Overprinting: When printing one colour on top of another the resulting third colour is called an overprint.

Table adhesives: These are special gum preparations for sticking cloth to the printing table.

Pulling through: The action of drawing the dye across the screen with a squeegee is called 'pulling through'.

Appendix

Fig. 114 Screen printed fabric based on plant drawings

Basic equipment necessary for screen printing and designing

1 Table
2 Padding
3 Table coverings
4 Table adhesives
   a) Gum Arabic   From any good art materials store and Harrington Bros. Ltd., Weir Road, Balham, SW12.
   b) Lankro   (Available only in Great Britain) Head Office, Lankro Chemicals, 12, Whitehall, London, SW1.
   c) Sellotape (Scotch Tape)
   d) Masking tape
5 Screen frames
6 Organdie
7 Staple gun, staples
8 Squeegees
9 Brown gummed paper

Dyestuffs and commercial products with list of suppliers

Tinolite pigment dyes	Marketed by Winsor and Newton under the name Printex Dyes in UK and in the USA by Geigy Chemical Co. Yonkers, New York, under the name Tinolite Pigments. In the USA, Tinolite is available only in large quantities.
Helizarin dyes	Skilbeck Bros Bagnall House, 55-57 Glengall Road, SE15 (UK). Accolite Pigments, American Crayon Company, Sandusky, Ohio (USA).
Dylon Dyes (UK) Tintex Dyes (USA) Basic dye 'Rex' cold water paste, or any wallpaper paste.	Also from Skilbeck Bros.

Shellac	(The solvent is methylated spirits—alcohol). Any paint or hardware store.
Copal varnish	(The solvent is turps. substitute) Any good art material store.
Cellulose lacquer (black)	(UK) The solvent is lacquer thinner.
Silk screen block out lacquer	(USA) Any paint or hardware store.
Screen printing inks	John T. Keep and Sons Ltd. (UK) 15, Theobalds Road, WC1. Screen Process Supplies, 1199 East 12 Street, Oakland, California 94606 (USA) Naz-Dar Co. 33 Lafayette Ave., Brooklyn, New York 11217.
Profilm	Screen Process Supplies Ltd,
Kodatrace	24 Parsons Green Lane, SW6.
Photopake	Screen Process Supplies, 1199 East 12 Street, Oakland California 94606 (USA).

Designing materials

Variety of papers
  a) Cartridge (drawing) paper
  b) Newsprint
  c) Coloured papers
  d) Coloured tissue paper
Paint brushes—assorted
  a) Hoghair (bristle) and sable
  b) 2″ wide decorator's brush
  c) 4″ wide decorator's brush
Coloured chalks
Coloured wax crayons
Candles
Paraffin wax
Poster paints
Pencils
Rulers
Yardstick

Assorted waste materials—
  match boxes, cotton reels
  (spools), bottle tops etc.
Potatoes
Water bound (base) printing inks
Photographic squeegee roller
String
Felt
Lino (cutting tools)
Wood blocks
Glass (from old photographs or
  window panes)
Household starch
Household bleach
Pipe cleaners
Ink
Pens

Cow Gum (rubber cement)
Drawing pins
Evostick or Bostik (UK)

Elmer's Glue or Sobo (USA)
semi-permanent waterproof
glue

Useful kitchen equipment

Measuring spoons
Pint measure
Saucepans
Plastic or enamel basins
Double boiler
Screw topped jars

Rubber spatula
Fork or egg whisk
Sink
Double hose pipe
Iron
Rags and newspapers

For further reading

Principles and Practice of Textile Printing by E. Knecht and J. Fothergill. Charles Griffin and Co. Ltd, London.
Fabric Printing by hand by Stephen Russ. Studio Vista, London.
An Introduction to Textile Printing. Butterworths, London (in association with I.C.I. dyestuffs division).
Printed Textile Design by Terence Conran. Studio Publications, London and New York.

Suggested books for designing
Formen Des Mikrokosmos by Carl Strüwe. Prestel-Verlag, Munchen. F. Lewis Publishers Ltd, Leigh-on-Sea.
Urformen der Kunst by Professor Karl Blossfeldt. Verlag-Ernst Wasmuth, Tübingen.
Designs for Craftsmen by Walter Miles. Doubleday, New York. G. Bell and Sons Ltd, London.
A Handbook of Ornament by Franz S. Meyer. Dover Publications Inc. New York.

Index

Acknowledgements

The authors wish to acknowledge the work of the Students of The London College of Furniture.

The photographs are by Brian Boothby.

Permission to reproduce the section on 'Possible sources of trouble in screen making' (page 92) from An Introduction to Textile Printing, published by Butterworths in association with I.C.I. Dyestuffs Division, is gratefully acknowledged.

Fig. 115 Indian block print